30

Spicy
Foods

30 MINUTES OR LESS | Spicy Foods

p

This is a Parragon Publishing Book

First published in 2006

Parragon Publishing

Queen Street House

4 Queen Street

Bath BA1 1HE, UK

ISBN: 1-40547-308-8

Printed in China

Produced by the Bridgewater Book Company Ltd

Front cover photography by Mike Cooper

Front cover home economy by Sumi Glass

Notes for the Reader

This book uses imperial, metric, and US cup measurements. Follow the same units of measurement

throughout; do not mix imperial and metric. All spoon measurements are level: teaspoons are

assumed to be 5 ml, and tablespoons are assumed to be 15 ml. Unless otherwise stated,

milk is assumed to be whole milk, eggs and individual vegetables are medium, and pepper is

freshly ground black pepper.

Recipes using raw or very lightly cooked eggs should be avoided by infants, the elderly,

pregnant women, convalescents, and anyone suffering from an illness. Pregnant women and

breast-feeding women are advised to avoid eating peanuts and peanut products.

Contents

Introduction 6

Chapter One
Appetizers and Snacks 8

Chapter Two
Fish and Seafood 30

Chapter Three
Meat 52

Chapter Four
Vegetarian 74

Index 96

Introduction

Sometimes even the most creative cook needs to spice up the menu, and there's nothing like a fiery flavor to brighten up the blandest of foods. This fabulous and inspiring selection of flavorsome and exotic dishes is a source of inspiration for anyone who enjoys eating spicy foods.

Written for anyone who enjoys eating spicy food but doesn't want to spend hours in the kitchen, these easy recipes have been specially chosen so that even the busiest person can enjoy delicious, fresh, home-cooked food, and quickly, too. All the recipes in this book can be completed in 30 minutes or under, or about the time it takes to heat through a supermarket ready meal. The recipes are all designed to be executed with the minimum of time and effort—there are no complicated cooking methods or elaborate presentations, nor will you need to use every pot and pan in the kitchen. Simple step-by-step directions and full-color photographs enable even the most inexperienced to cook with confidence and success.

The book is divided into four chapters: appetizers and snacks, fish and seafood, meat, and vegetarian. Recipes have been inspired by cuisines around the world, drawing on an astonishing range of tastes, and are guaranteed to satisfy even the most ardent fan of fiery foods or those who prefer rather more subtle, tangy aromas.

Most cultures have their own way of making foods sizzle with flavor and excitement. Even the most calorie-restrictive diet can be enhanced with spicy foods. And hot foods often mean healthy foods—there are numerous health benefits—from reduced blood pressure to lower cholesterol levels—associated with eating garlic or chiles. As an added bonus,

spicy cooking masks the flavor of some nutrient-rich foods that many people find unpalatable, such as spinach or soy, so you can reap their health benefits without having to endure their tastes.

SPICY PANTRY STAPLES

Don't rely on an ancient bottle of Tabasco sauce to tickle your taste buds—stock up on these key ingredients and you'll be able to whip up a sizzling, steamy, and irresistible meal at the drop of a hat. There is an incredible variety of chiles, herbs, and spices that you can use to create luscious flavors—just add, subtract, or even substitute to suit your personal preferences.

DRIED CHILES, HERBS, AND SPICES

In an ideal world, all herbs and spices should be fresh, but in reality, this isn't always possible. Buy dried herbs and spices in small quantities because they become stale quite quickly, and keep them out of sunlight. Here are a few suggestions for herbs and spices to keep in stock:

Black peppercorns

Cardamom (green pods)

Cayenne pepper

Chinese five-spice powder

Chiles (whole and/or crushed) and chili powder

Cilantro and coriander

Cinnamon (whole and ground)

Cloves (whole and ground)

Cumin (whole and ground)

Garam masala (Indian spice mix)

Kaffir lime leaves

Mace (ground)

Nutmeg (whole)

Paprika

Turmeric

Try to keep a supply of fresh gingerroot, galangal (if you can find it), Thai chiles (and any other varieties you like), lemongrass stems, and fresh cilantro in the freezer. To make the most of mustard, you'll need seeds, powder, and paste. Bottled ingredients with a kick should include pimientos (peppers), Thai green curry paste, Thai red curry paste, and Tabasco sauce.

If you want to create authentic and exciting recipes, you'll also need to stock up on Thai fish sauce, soy sauce, coconut milk, sesame oil, and ghee (clarified butter), and maintain a constant supply of lemons, limes, garlic, and shallots or onions. And make sure you've got a good range of grains and pasta in your pantry to offset those fiery flavors.

Turn up the heat on your everyday cooking with these easy-to-make, fun-to-eat, spicy favorites from around the world. Whether it's Mexican Eggs, Asian-Style Seafood Curry, or some Hot Chile Pasta, you'll discover radiant flavors and enticing tastes.

Chapter One
Appetizers and Snacks

Spicy Crab Soup
25 minutes to the table

SERVES 4

ingredients

4 cups chicken stock

2 tomatoes, skinned and
  finely chopped (see cook's tip)

1-inch/2.5-cm piece fresh gingerroot,
  finely chopped

1 small fresh red chile, seeded and
  finely chopped

2 tbsp Chinese rice wine

1 tbsp rice vinegar

¾ tsp sugar

1 tbsp cornstarch

2 tbsp water

6 oz/175 g white crabmeat, thawed
  if frozen or drained if canned

salt and pepper

2 scallions, shredded, to garnish

method

Pour the stock into a large, heavy-bottomed pot and add the tomatoes, gingerroot, chile, rice wine, vinegar, and sugar. Bring to a boil, then reduce the heat and simmer, covered, for 10 minutes.

Blend the cornstarch and water together in a pitcher, then stir into the soup. Simmer, stirring constantly, for 2 minutes, or until the soup thickens slightly.

Gently stir in the crabmeat and heat through for 2 minutes. Season to taste with salt and pepper, then ladle into warmed soup bowls and serve immediately, garnished with the shredded scallions.

cook's tip

Remove the skins of tomatoes by filling a pan with water and bringing it to a boil. Add the tomatoes and the skin will start to separate. Plunge the tomatoes into cold water and the skin will easily start to pull away.

variation

Chinese rice wine and rice vinegar are available from some large supermarkets as well as from Chinese food stores. If Chinese rice wine is not available, then use the same amount of dry sherry instead and replace the rice vinegar with white wine vinegar.

Omelet Rolls
20 minutes to the table

MAKES 8

ingredients

4 large eggs

2 tbsp water

1 tbsp Thai soy sauce

6 scallions, finely chopped

1 fresh red chile, seeded and
   finely chopped

1 tbsp vegetable oil or peanut oil

1 tbsp Thai green curry paste

bunch of fresh cilantro, chopped
   (2 sprigs reserved for garnish)

method

Beat the eggs, water, and soy sauce together in a bowl. Set aside. Put the scallions and chile in a mortar and pound to a paste with a pestle.

Heat half the oil in an 8-inch/20-cm skillet over medium heat. Pour in half the egg mixture. Tilt to coat the bottom of the pan evenly and cook until set. Lift out and set aside. Heat the remaining oil in the pan and make a second omelet in the same way.

Spread half the scallion and chili paste, and half the curry paste, in a thin layer over each omelet and sprinkle the chopped cilantro on top. Roll up tightly. Cut each roll in half and then cut each piece diagonally in half again. Serve immediately, while still warm, garnished with the cilantro sprigs.

Crispy Spring Rolls
30 minutes to the table

method

Heat the oil in a preheated wok or large skillet over high heat. Add the scallions and chile and stir-fry for 30 seconds. Add the carrot, zucchini, and red bell pepper and stir-fry for 1 minute. Remove from heat and stir in the bean sprouts, bamboo shoots, soy sauce, and chili sauce. Taste and add more soy sauce or chili sauce, if necessary.

Lay a spring roll skin on a clean counter and spoon some of the vegetable mixture diagonally across the center. Roll one corner over the filling and flip the sides of the skin over the top, to enclose the filling. Continue to roll up to make an enclosed package. Repeat with the remaining skins and filling to make 8 spring rolls.

Heat the oil for deep-frying in a preheated wok or large skillet to 350-375°F/180-190°C, or until a cube of bread browns in 30 seconds. Add the spring rolls, in 2 batches, and cook, until crisp and golden brown. Remove with a slotted spoon and then drain on paper towels, keeping them hot while you cook the remaining spring rolls. Serve immediately.

MAKES 8

ingredients

2 tbsp vegetable oil or peanut oil, plus extra for deep-frying

6 scallions, cut into 2-inch/5-cm lengths

1 fresh green chile, seeded and chopped

1 carrot, cut into thin batons

1 zucchini, cut into thin batons

½ red bell pepper, seeded and thinly sliced

generous ¾ cup bean sprouts, drained and rinsed if canned

4 oz/115 g canned bamboo shoots, drained and rinsed

3 tbsp Thai soy sauce

1-2 tbsp chili sauce

8 spring roll skins

Spicy Beef and Noodle Soup

20 minutes to the table

SERVES 4

ingredients

4 cups beef stock

²⁄₃ cup vegetable oil or
    peanut oil

3 oz/85 g dried rice vermicelli noodles

2 shallots, thinly sliced

2 garlic cloves, crushed

1-inch/2.5-cm piece fresh gingerroot,
    thinly sliced

8 oz/225 g tenderloin steak, cut into
    thin strips

2 tbsp Thai green curry paste

2 tbsp Thai soy sauce

1 tbsp Thai fish sauce

chopped fresh cilantro, to garnish

method

Pour the stock into a large pot and bring to a boil. Meanwhile, heat the oil in a preheated wok or large skillet. Add about one-third of the noodles and cook, stirring, for 10–20 seconds, or until puffed up. Lift out with tongs, drain on paper towels, and then set aside. Pour off all but 2 tablespoons of the oil from the wok.

Add the shallots, garlic, and gingerroot to the wok, and stir-fry for 1 minute. Add the beef and curry paste and stir-fry for 3–4 minutes, or until tender.

Transfer the beef mixture to the pot of stock with the uncooked noodles, and the soy sauce and fish sauce. Simmer for 2–3 minutes, or until the noodles have swelled. Serve hot, garnished with chopped cilantro and the reserved crispy noodles.

Scallops on Noodles
20 minutes to the table

method

Cook the noodles in a large pan of boiling water for 1½ minutes, or according to the package directions, until tender, then rinse under cold running water and drain well. Meanwhile, melt the butter in a small pan over low heat. Add the garlic and cook, stirring, for 1 minute. Stir in the paprika and set aside.

Heat the oil in a preheated wok or large skillet over high heat. Stir in the curry paste, water, and soy sauce and bring to a boil. Add the cooked noodles and reheat, stirring gently. Stir in the scallions, then remove from the heat and keep warm.

Heat a ridged, cast-iron grill pan over high heat and brush lightly with oil. Add the scallops to the pan and cook, brushing with the garlic butter, for 3 minutes, then turn over and cook for no more than 2 minutes on the other side, or until just cooked (the centers shouldn't be totally opaque if cut open). Season to taste with salt and pepper. Divide the noodles between 4 individual dishes and top with 3 scallops each. Garnish with scallion slices.

cook's tip

This is an excellent dish to serve at a dinner party, but you have to be organized. You can boil the noodles and make the garlic butter for cooking the scallops ahead of time, but, since everything else is done at the last minute, it's a good idea to have your guests seated when you start cooking. You want the scallops to go from the pan to the table as quickly as possible.

SERVES 4

ingredients

4 oz/115 g dried green tea noodles, or the thinnest green noodles you can find

2 tbsp butter

1 garlic clove, crushed

pinch of paprika

1 tbsp peanut oil or sunflower-seed oil, plus extra for brushing

2 tbsp Thai green curry paste

2 tbsp water

2 tsp light soy sauce

2 scallions, finely shredded, plus extra, sliced, to garnish

12 fresh raw scallops, shucked

salt and pepper

Indonesian Corn Balls

20 minutes to the table

SERVES 4

ingredients

generous ¾ cup unsalted peanuts

scant 3 cups canned corn kernels,
 drained

1 onion, finely chopped

generous ¾ cup all-purpose flour

1 tsp ground coriander

½ tsp sambal oelek or chili sauce

1-2 tbsp warm water (optional)

peanut oil, for deep-frying

salt

method

Put the peanuts in a food processor and process briefly, until coarsely ground. Alternatively, grind them in a mortar with a pestle. Transfer to a bowl and stir in the corn kernels, onion, flour, coriander, and sambal oelek. Season to taste with salt. Knead to a dough, adding the warm water, if necessary, to make the dough workable.

Heat the oil in a deep-fryer or large, heavy-bottomed pan to 350-375°F/180-190°C, or until a cube of bread browns in 30 seconds. Using your hands, form tablespoonfuls of the dough into balls. Add the corn balls to the pan, in batches, and cook until golden and crisp.

Remove with a slotted spoon, then drain on paper towels and keep hot while you cook the remaining corn balls. Serve immediately or let cool before serving.

cook's tip

Sambal oelek is a fiery-hot chili sauce available from Asian food stores and supermarkets. If you cannot find it, use chili sauce instead.

Whitebait with Green Chili Sauce

20 minutes to the table

method

Cook the fish in a large pan of boiling water for between 30 seconds and 2 minutes, or until the flesh is turning soft but not breaking up. Drain and let cool.

Meanwhile, to make the sauce, heat the oil in a small pan over high heat, until smoking. Add the chile and cook, turning frequently, until the skin blisters. Remove and let cool. When cool enough to handle, peel off the skin and finely chop the flesh. Let cool, then mix with all the other sauce ingredients in a bowl.

To serve, pour the sauce over the fish and serve immediately.

cook's tip

These fish have a tendency to stick together and break easily once cooked, so treat with care.

SERVES 4

ingredients

6 oz/175 g whitebait

SAUCE
1 tbsp vegetable oil or peanut oil
1 large fresh green chile
2 drops of sesame oil
1 tbsp light soy sauce
pinch of salt
pinch of sugar
1 garlic clove, finely chopped

Mexican Eggs
20 minutes to the table

SERVES 4

ingredients

8 large eggs

2 tbsp milk

1 tsp olive oil

1 red bell pepper, seeded and thinly
    sliced

½ fresh red chile, finely chopped

1 fresh chorizo sausage, outer casing
    removed, sliced

4 tbsp chopped fresh cilantro

pepper

4 slices toasted whole-wheat bread,
    to serve

method

Beat the eggs, milk, and pepper to taste together in a large bowl, then set aside.

Heat the oil in a nonstick skillet over medium heat. Add the red bell pepper and chile and cook, stirring frequently, for 5 minutes, or until the red bell pepper is softened and browned in places. Add the chorizo and cook, stirring frequently, until just browned. Transfer to a warmed plate and set aside.

Return the pan to the heat, then add the egg mixture, and cook, stirring with a wooden spoon, to a soft scramble. Add the chorizo mixture and stir to combine, then scatter over the cilantro.

Serve immediately on toasted whole-wheat bread.

Chorizo Empanadillas
30 minutes to the table

MAKES 12

ingredients

9 oz/250 g ready-made puff pastry,
    thawed if frozen
all-purpose flour, for dusting
4½ oz/125 g cured chorizo sausage,
    outer casing removed, cut into
    ½-inch/1-cm dice
beaten egg, to glaze
paprika, to garnish

method

Preheat the oven to 400°F/200°C. Sprinkle 2 baking sheets with water.

Roll out the pie dough thinly on a lightly floured counter. Using a plain, round 3¼-inch/8-cm cutter, cut out 12 circles. Put about a teaspoon of the diced chorizo onto one half of each pie dough circle.

Dampen the edge of each pie dough circle with a little water, then fold the plain half over the chorizo to cover. Seal the edges together with your fingers. Using the prongs of a fork, press against the edges to give a decorative finish and seal them farther. With the tip of a sharp knife, make a small slit in the side of each empanadilla. You can store the empanadillas, covered with plastic wrap, in the refrigerator at this stage, until you are ready to bake.

Transfer the empanadillas to the prepared baking sheets and brush each with a little beaten egg to glaze. Bake in the preheated oven for 10–15 minutes, or until golden brown and well risen. Using a small sifter, lightly dust the top of each empanadilla with paprika to garnish. Serve the empanadillas hot or warm.

cook's tip

Serve as delicious tapas with glasses of chilled white wine.

Asian Seafood Soup
30 minutes to the table

method

Heat the oil in a large pan over medium heat. Add the garlic, chiles, lemongrass, and gingerroot, and cook, stirring frequently, for 5 minutes. Add the stock and bring to a boil, then reduce the heat and simmer for 5 minutes.

Stir in the shrimp, mushrooms, and carrot. If using the egg noodles, break into small lengths, then add to the pan and simmer for another 5 minutes, or until the shrimp have turned pink and the noodles are just tender.

Stir in the fish sauce and cilantro and heat through for another minute before serving.

variation

Use a package of mixed Asian mushrooms in place of the shiitake mushrooms, if available.

SERVES 4

ingredients

1 tbsp sunflower-seed oil

2–3 garlic cloves, cut into thin slivers

1–2 fresh red Thai chiles, seeded and sliced

2 lemongrass stems, outer leaves removed, chopped

1-inch/2.5-cm piece fresh gingerroot, grated

5 cups fish stock or vegetable stock

12 oz/350 g large raw shrimp, shelled and deveined

4 oz/115 g shiitake mushrooms, sliced

1 large carrot, grated

2 oz/55 g dried egg noodles (optional)

1–2 tsp Thai fish sauce

1 tbsp chopped fresh cilantro

Chapter Two
Fish and Seafood

Chiles Stuffed with Fish Paste

30 minutes to the table

method

Mix all the ingredients for the marinade together in a bowl. Add the fish and toss to coat in the marinade. Cover with plastic wrap and let marinate in a cool place while you prepare the other ingredients.

Cut the chiles in half lengthwise and scoop out the seeds and white veins. Cut into bite-size pieces.

Add the egg to the fish mixture and mix to a smooth paste. Spread each piece of chile with about ½ teaspoon of the fish mixture. Heat the oil in a preheated wok or deep pan over high heat. Add the chile pieces and cook on both sides, until beginning to brown. Remove with a slotted spoon and drain on paper towels.

Pour off all but 1 tablespoon of the oil from the wok, and heat over high heat. Add the garlic and stir-fry for 1 minute, or until fragrant. Stir in the beans and mix well. Stir in the soy sauce and sugar, then add the chile pieces. Add the water, then cover and simmer over low heat for 5 minutes. Serve immediately.

variation

This dish can also be made with bitter melon (sometimes known as balsam pear), which should be prepared in the same way as the chiles, but must be blanched before being topped with the fish paste.

SERVES 4-6

ingredients

8 oz/225 g white fish, ground
4-6 fresh mild red and green chiles
2 tbsp lightly beaten egg
vegetable oil or peanut oil, for
    shallow-frying
2 garlic cloves, finely chopped
½ tbsp fermented black beans, rinsed
    and lightly mashed
1 tbsp light soy sauce
pinch of sugar
1 tbsp water

MARINADE
1 tsp finely chopped fresh gingerroot
pinch of salt
pinch of white pepper
½ tsp vegetable oil or peanut oil

Fish Curry with Rice Noodles

25 minutes to the table

SERVES 4-6

ingredients

2 tbsp vegetable oil or peanut oil

1 large onion, chopped

2 garlic cloves, chopped

3 oz/85 g white mushrooms

8 oz/225 g skinless angler fish fillet,
    cut into 1-inch/2.5-cm cubes

8 oz/225 g skinless salmon fillet,
    cut into 1-inch/2.5-cm cubes

8 oz/225 g skinless cod fillet,
    cut into 1-inch/2.5-cm cubes

2 tbsp Thai red curry paste

1¾ cups canned coconut milk

handful of fresh cilantro, chopped

1 tsp jaggery or soft light
    brown sugar

1 tsp Thai fish sauce

4 oz/115 g dried rice noodles

3 scallions, chopped

⅓ cup fresh bean sprouts

handful of fresh Thai basil sprigs

method

Heat the oil in a preheated wok or large skillet over medium heat. Add the onion, garlic, and mushrooms, and cook, stirring frequently, for 5 minutes, or until softened but not browned.

Add all the fish, curry paste, and coconut milk, and bring slowly to a boil. Reduce the heat and simmer for 2-3 minutes. Stir in half the cilantro, and all the jaggery and fish sauce. Set aside and keep warm.

Meanwhile, soak the noodles in a pan of just-boiled water for 3-4 minutes, or according to the package directions, until tender, then drain well using a colander. Set the colander and noodles over a pan of simmering water. Add the scallions, bean sprouts, and most of the basil, and steam on top of the noodles for 1-2 minutes, or until just wilted.

Pile the noodles onto warmed serving plates and top with the fish curry. Scatter the remaining cilantro over the top, then garnish with the remaining basil sprigs and serve immediately.

cook's tip

Coconut milk is used frequently in Thai curries, to flavor and enrich them. It is not, however, as one might think, the liquid inside a coconut. Coconut milk is actually made from the flesh of fresh coconut, which is grated and pressed and then combined with water.

Wok-Fried Jumbo Shrimp in Spicy Sauce

20 minutes to the table

SERVES 4

ingredients

3 tbsp vegetable oil or peanut oil

1 lb/450 g raw jumbo shrimp, deveined
   but unshelled

2 tsp finely chopped fresh gingerroot

1 tsp finely chopped garlic

1 tbsp chopped scallion

2 tbsp chili bean sauce

1 tsp Chinese rice wine

1 tsp sugar

½ tsp light soy sauce

1-2 tbsp chicken stock

method

Heat the oil in a preheated wok or deep pan over high heat. Add the shrimp and stir-fry for 4 minutes. Push the shrimp up the side of the wok out of the oil, then add the gingerroot and garlic and stir-fry for 1 minute, or until fragrant. Add the scallion and chili bean sauce, and stir in the shrimp.

Reduce the heat slightly and add the rice wine, sugar, soy sauce, and stock. Cover and cook for another minute. Serve immediately.

cook's tip

Increase the amount of chili bean sauce to create a hotter dish, if you prefer.

Tagliatelle with Hake in Chili Sauce

25 minutes to the table

method

Using a sharp knife, chop the parsley, garlic, and chile together. Heat half the oil in a large, heavy-bottomed skillet over low heat. Add the herb mixture and cook, stirring, for 1–2 minutes, or until the garlic is fragrant. Add the fish, then cover the pan and cook for 5 minutes, then turn the fish and cook for another 5 minutes. Add the tomatoes and season to taste with salt and pepper, then re-cover and simmer for another 5 minutes.

Meanwhile, bring a large, heavy-bottomed pan of lightly salted water to a boil. Add the pasta, return to a boil, and cook for 8–10 minutes, or according to the package instructions, until tender but still firm to the bite.

Drain the pasta and return to the pan. Drizzle with the remaining oil and toss to coat. Transfer to a warmed serving platter and top with the fish mixture. Serve immediately.

cook's tip

Make sure that you remove any fine bones remaining in the fish fillets. This is most easily done with tweezers.

SERVES 4

ingredients

bunch of fresh parsley

1 garlic clove

1 dried red chile, seeded

5 tbsp olive oil

1 lb/450 g hake fillets, skinned and cut into chunks

12 oz/350 g tomatoes, skinned, seeded, and diced

12 oz/350 g dried tagliatelle

salt and pepper

Shrimp and Pineapple Curry

20 minutes to the table

SERVES 4

ingredients

scant 2 cups coconut cream

½ fresh pineapple, peeled, cored,
    and chopped

2 tbsp Thai red curry paste

2 tbsp Thai fish sauce

2 tsp sugar

12 oz/350 g raw jumbo shrimp, shelled
    and deveined

2 tbsp chopped fresh cilantro, plus
    extra to garnish

jasmine rice, to serve

method

Heat the coconut cream, pineapple, curry paste, fish sauce, and sugar in a pan over medium heat, until almost boiling. Stir in the shrimp and cilantro, then reduce the heat and simmer gently for 3 minutes, or until the shrimp have turned pink.

   Sprinkle with extra cilantro and serve immediately with cooked jasmine rice.

Scallops in Black Bean Sauce

15 minutes to the table

SERVES 4

ingredients

2 tbsp vegetable oil or peanut oil

1 tsp finely chopped garlic

1 tsp finely chopped fresh gingerroot

1 tbsp fermented black beans, rinsed and lightly mashed

14 oz/400 g fresh raw scallops, shucked

½ tsp light soy sauce

1 tsp Chinese rice wine

1 tsp sugar

3–4 fresh red Thai chiles, finely chopped

1–2 tsp chicken stock

1 tbsp finely chopped scallion

method

Heat the oil in a preheated wok or deep pan over high heat. Add the garlic and stir, then add the gingerroot and stir-fry together for 1 minute, or until fragrant. Mix in the beans and toss in the scallops, then stir-fry for 1 minute. Add the soy sauce, rice wine, sugar, and chiles.

Reduce the heat and simmer for 2 minutes, adding the stock if necessary. Add the scallion and stir, then serve immediately.

cook's tip

Fresh scallops, removed from their shells, are always preferable, but frozen scallops also work well in this strongly flavored dish.

Mussels with Mustard Seeds and Shallots

30 minutes to the table

method

Discard any mussels with broken shells or any that refuse to close when tapped.

Heat the oil in a preheated kadhai, wok, or large skillet over medium-high heat. Add the mustard seeds and cook, stirring, for 1 minute, or until beginning to jump.

Add the shallots and garlic and cook, stirring frequently, for 3 minutes, or until beginning to brown. Stir in the vinegar, chiles, dissolved creamed coconut, curry leaves, turmeric, chili powder, and a pinch of salt, and bring to a boil, stirring.

Reduce the heat to very low. Add the mussels, then cover the pan and simmer, shaking the pan frequently, for 3-4 minutes, or until the mussels are opened. Discard any that remain closed. Ladle the mussels into deep bowls, then taste the sauce and add extra salt, if necessary. Spoon the sauce over the mussels and serve immediately.

cook's tip

Peeling a large number of shallots can be time-consuming, but the job is quicker if you submerge them beforehand in a pan of boiling water for 30-45 seconds. Drain the shallots and use a knife to slice off the root end, then they should peel easily.

SERVES 4

ingredients

4 lb 8 oz/2 kg live mussels, scrubbed and debearded

3 tbsp vegetable oil or peanut oil

½ tbsp black mustard seeds

8 shallots, chopped (see cook's tip)

2 garlic cloves, crushed

2 tbsp distilled vinegar

4 small fresh red chiles

3 oz/85 g creamed coconut, grated and dissolved in 1¼ cups boiling water

10 fresh curry leaves or 1 tbsp dried

½ tsp ground turmeric

¼-½ tsp chili powder

salt

Asian-Style Seafood Curry

30 minutes to the table

SERVES 4-6

ingredients

3 tbsp vegetable oil or peanut oil

1 tbsp black mustard seeds

12 fresh curry leaves or 1 tbsp dried

6 shallots, finely chopped

1 garlic clove, crushed

1 tsp ground turmeric

½ tsp ground coriander

¼-½ tsp chili powder

5 oz/140 g creamed coconut, grated
   and dissolved in 1¼ cups boiling
   water

1 lb 2 oz/500 g skinless white fish
   fillets, such as angler fish or cod,
   cut into large chunks

1 lb/450 g large raw shrimp, shelled
   and deveined

juice and finely grated zest of 1 lime

salt

lime wedges, to serve

method

Heat the oil in a preheated kadhai, wok, or large skillet over high heat. Add the mustard seeds and cook, stirring, for 1 minute, or until they begin to jump. Stir in the curry leaves.

Add the shallots and garlic and cook, stirring frequently, for 5 minutes, or until the shallots are golden. Stir in the turmeric, coriander, and chili powder, and cook, stirring, for 30 seconds.

Add the dissolved creamed coconut. Bring to a boil, then reduce the heat to medium and cook, stirring, for 2 minutes.

Reduce the heat to low, then add the fish and simmer for 1 minute, spooning the sauce over the fish, and very gently stirring it around. Add the shrimp and simmer for another 4-5 minutes, or until the fish flesh flakes easily and the shrimp have turned pink.

Add half the lime juice, then taste and add more lime juice and salt to taste. Sprinkle with the lime zest and serve with lime wedges.

Crab and Cilantro Salad

15 minutes to the table

method

Put the crabmeat in a bowl and stir in the scallions and cilantro.

Mix all the ingredients for the dressing together in a pitcher.
Arrange the shredded lettuce on a serving platter and scatter with
the cucumber.

Arrange the crab salad over the lettuce and drizzle the dressing over
the salad. Serve immediately.

SERVES 4

ingredients
12 oz/350 g canned
    white crabmeat, drained
4 scallions, finely chopped
handful of fresh cilantro, chopped,
    plus extra sprigs to garnish
1 head Webbs lettuce, shredded
3-inch/7.5-cm piece cucumber,
    chopped

DRESSING
1 garlic clove, crushed
1-inch/2.5-cm piece gingerroot,
    grated
2 lime leaves, torn into pieces
juice of 1 lime
1 tsp Thai fish sauce

Malaysian-Style Coconut Noodles with Shrimp

25 minutes to the table

SERVES 4

ingredients

2 tbsp vegetable oil

1 small red bell pepper, seeded
    and diced

7 oz/200 g bok choy, stems thinly
    sliced and leaves chopped

2 large garlic cloves, chopped

1 tsp ground turmeric

2 tsp garam masala

1 tsp chili powder (optional)

½ cup hot vegetable stock

2 heaping tbsp smooth peanut butter

1½ cups coconut milk

1 tbsp tamari (thick, dark, wheat-free
    soy sauce)

9 oz/250 g dried rice noodles

10 oz/280 g large cooked
    shelled shrimp

TO GARNISH

2 scallions, finely shredded

1 tbsp sesame seeds

method

Heat the oil in a preheated wok or large, heavy-bottomed skillet over high heat. Add the red bell pepper, bok choy stems, and garlic, and stir-fry for 3 minutes. Add the turmeric, garam masala, chili powder if using, and bok choy leaves, and stir-fry for another minute.

Mix the hot stock and the peanut butter together in a heatproof bowl, until the peanut butter has dissolved, then add to the stir-fry with the coconut milk and tamari. Cook over medium heat for 5 minutes, or until reduced and thickened.

Meanwhile, soak the noodles in a pan of just-boiled water for 3-4 minutes, or according to the package instructions, until tender, then drain and refresh the noodles under cold running water. Add the noodles and shrimp to the curry and cook, stirring frequently, for another 2-3 minutes, or until heated through.

Serve the noodle dish immediately, sprinkled with the shredded scallions and the sesame seeds.

Chapter Three
Meat

Pepperoni Pasta

25 minutes to the table

SERVES 4

ingredients

3 tbsp olive oil

1 onion, chopped

1 red bell pepper, seeded and diced

1 orange bell pepper, seeded and diced

1 lb 12 oz/800 g canned
    chopped tomatoes in juice

1 tbsp sun-dried tomato paste

1 tsp paprika

8 oz/225 g pepperoni sausage, sliced

2 tbsp chopped fresh flat-leaf parsley,
    plus extra to garnish

1 lb/450 g dried garganelli pasta

salt and pepper

mixed salad greens, to serve

method

Heat 2 tablespoons of the oil in a large, heavy-bottomed skillet over medium heat. Add the onion and cook, stirring occasionally, for 5 minutes, or until softened. Stir in the red and orange bell peppers, tomatoes with their juice, sun-dried tomato paste, and paprika, and bring to a boil.

Add the pepperoni and parsley, and season to taste with salt and pepper. Stir well and bring to a boil, then reduce the heat and simmer for 10-15 minutes.

Meanwhile, bring a large, heavy-bottomed pan of lightly salted water to a boil. Add the pasta, then return to a boil and cook for 8-10 minutes, or according to the package directions, until tender but still firm to the bite. Drain well and transfer to a warmed serving dish. Add the remaining oil and toss to coat. Add the sauce and toss again. Sprinkle with parsley to garnish and serve immediately with mixed salad greens.

variation

If you cannot find garganelli pasta, then use penne or another pasta shape, such as fusilli bucati or farfalle.

cook's tip

Pepperoni is a hotly spiced Italian sausage made from pork and beef, and is flavored with fennel. You could substitute other spicy sausages, such as kabanos or chorizo, if you prefer.

Spicy Beef
30 minutes to the table

SERVES 4

ingredients

8 oz/225 g tenderloin steak
2 garlic cloves, crushed
1 tsp ground star anise
1 tbsp dark soy sauce

SAUCE
2 tbsp vegetable oil
bunch of scallions,
    halved lengthwise
1 tbsp dark soy sauce
1 tbsp dry sherry
¼ tsp chili sauce
⅔ cup water
2 tsp cornstarch
4 tsp water

method

Cut the steak into thin strips and put in a shallow dish.

Mix the garlic, star anise, and soy sauce together in a small bowl, and pour over the steak strips, turning to coat in the marinade. Cover with plastic wrap and marinate at room temperature for 15 minutes.

Heat the oil in a preheated wok or large skillet over high heat. Reduce the heat, then add the halved scallions and stir-fry for 1-2 minutes. Remove from the wok with a slotted spoon and set aside.

Add the beef to the wok, together with the marinade, and stir-fry for 3-4 minutes. Return the halved scallions to the wok and add the soy sauce, sherry, chili sauce, and two-thirds of the water.

Blend the cornstarch with the remaining water in a pitcher and stir into the wok. Bring to a boil and cook, stirring constantly, until the sauce thickens and clears.

Transfer to a warmed serving dish and serve immediately.

Stir-Fried Lamb
25 minutes to the table

method

Heat the oil in a preheated wok or large, heavy-bottomed skillet over high heat. Add the lamb and stir-fry for 2–3 minutes, or until browned all over. Remove with a slotted spoon and drain on paper towels.

Add the onion, garlic, and chiles to the wok, and stir-fry for 3 minutes. Add the snow peas and stir-fry for 2 minutes, then stir in the spinach leaves and return the lamb to the wok.

Add the lime juice, oyster sauce, fish sauce, and sugar, and cook, stirring constantly, for 4 minutes, or until the lamb is cooked through and tender. Stir in the mint and season to taste with salt and pepper, then serve immediately.

variations

Replace the lime juice with the same amount of lemon juice, and if you don't like it too hot, use just 1 fresh red chile.

cook's tip

Oyster sauce is a thick soy sauce, which is flavored with oyster juice. The taste is very delicate and is ideal for dishes that need livening up. It is found in most supermarkets and Chinese food stores.

SERVES 4

ingredients

4 tbsp peanut oil

1 lb 4 oz/550 g neck slice of lamb, thinly sliced

1 large onion, finely chopped

2 garlic cloves, finely chopped

2 fresh red chiles, seeded and thinly sliced

1¾ cups snow peas

12 oz/350 g fresh spinach leaves

2 tbsp lime juice

3 tbsp oyster sauce

2 tbsp Thai fish sauce

2 tsp superfine sugar

5 tbsp chopped fresh mint

salt and pepper

Grilled Steak with Hot Chili Salsa

20 minutes to the table

SERVES 4

ingredients

sunflower-seed or corn oil,
   for brushing
4 sirloin steaks, about 8 oz/
   225 g each
salt and pepper

HOT CHILI SALSA
4 fresh red habanero or Scotch
   bonnet chiles
4 fresh green poblano chiles
3 tomatoes, skinned, seeded,
   and diced
2 tbsp chopped fresh cilantro
1 tbsp red wine vinegar
2 tbsp olive oil
salt

method

To make the salsa, preheat the broiler to high. Arrange the chiles on a baking sheet and cook under the preheated broiler, turning frequently, until blackened and charred. Let cool. When cool enough to handle, peel off the skins. Halve and seed the chiles, then finely chop the flesh.

Mix the chiles, tomatoes, and cilantro together in a bowl. Whisk the vinegar and oil together in a pitcher, then season to taste with salt and pour over the salsa. Toss well, then cover with plastic wrap and chill in the refrigerator until required.

Heat a ridged, cast-iron grill pan over medium heat and brush lightly with oil. Season the steaks to taste with salt and pepper, then add to the grill pan and cook for 2-4 minutes on each side, or until cooked to your liking. Serve immediately with the salsa.

Pad Thai

25 minutes to the table

method

Soak the noodles in a pan of just-boiled water for 10 minutes, or until only just tender, then drain well and set aside.

Meanwhile, heat the oil in a wok or large skillet over high heat. Add the garlic, chiles, and pork, and stir-fry for 2-3 minutes. Add the shrimp and stir-fry for 2-3 minutes.

Add the garlic chives and noodles, then cover and heat through for 1-2 minutes. Add the fish sauce, lime juice, jaggery, and eggs, and cook, stirring and tossing constantly to mix in the eggs, for 2 minutes.

Stir in the bean sprouts, cilantro, and peanuts. Garnish with cilantro sprigs and extra chopped peanuts, and serve immediately with small dishes of crispy fried onions.

SERVES 4

ingredients

8 oz/225 g dried thick rice stick
    noodles
2 tbsp vegetable oil or peanut oil
2 garlic cloves, chopped
2 fresh red chiles, seeded and
    chopped
6 oz/175 g pork tenderloin, thinly
    sliced
4 oz/115 g raw shrimp, shelled,
    deveined, and chopped
8 fresh garlic chives, snipped
2 tbsp Thai fish sauce
juice of 1 lime
2 tsp jaggery or soft
    light brown sugar
2 eggs, beaten
generous ¾ cup fresh bean sprouts
4 tbsp chopped fresh cilantro, plus
    extra sprigs to garnish
generous ¾ cup unsalted peanuts,
    chopped, plus extra to serve
crispy pan-fried onions, to serve

Pork with Mixed Green Beans

20 minutes to the table

method

Heat the oil in a preheated wok or large skillet over high heat. Add the shallots, pork, galangal, and garlic, and stir-fry for 3-4 minutes, until the pork is lightly browned all over.

Add the stock, chili sauce, and peanut butter, and cook, stirring, or until the peanut butter has melted. Add all the beans, then stir well and simmer for 3-4 minutes, or until tender and the pork is cooked through. Serve immediately with crispy noodles.

SERVES 4

ingredients

2 tbsp vegetable oil or peanut oil

2 shallots, chopped

8 oz/225 g tenderloin fillet, thinly
    sliced

1-inch/2.5-cm piece fresh galangal or
    gingerroot, thinly sliced

2 garlic cloves, chopped

1¼ cups chicken stock

4 tbsp chili sauce

4 tbsp crunchy peanut butter

¾ cup fine green beans

1 cup frozen fava beans

¾ cup string beans, sliced

crispy noodles, to serve

Ground Chicken Skewers

20 minutes to the table

MAKES 8

ingredients

1 lb/450 g ground fresh chicken

1 onion, finely chopped

1 fresh red chile, seeded and chopped

2 tbsp Thai red curry paste

1 tsp jaggery or soft light brown sugar

1 tsp ground coriander

1 tsp ground cumin

1 egg white

8 lemongrass stems

cooked rice with chopped scallion,
    to serve

method

Mix the chicken, onion, chile, curry paste, and jaggery to a thick paste in a bowl. Stir in the coriander, cumin, and egg white, and mix again.

Preheat the broiler to high. Divide the mixture into 8 equal portions and squeeze them around each of the lemongrass stems. Arrange on a broiler rack and cook under the preheated broiler, turning frequently, for 8 minutes, or until browned and cooked through. Serve immediately, accompanied by cooked rice with chopped scallion stirred through it.

Stir-Fried Chicken with Thai Basil

25 minutes to the table

method

Heat the oil in a preheated wok or large skillet over high heat. Add the garlic and scallions and stir-fry for 1-2 minutes, or until the scallions are softened.

Add the chiles and green bell pepper and stir-fry for 2 minutes.

Add the chicken and stir-fry for 3-4 minutes, or until browned all over. Add the chopped Thai basil and the fish sauce and stir-fry for another 3-4 minutes, or until the chicken is cooked through. Garnish with basil sprigs and serve immediately with cooked rice.

SERVES 4

ingredients

2 tbsp vegetable oil

4 garlic cloves, crushed

4 scallions, finely chopped

4 fresh green chiles, seeded and finely chopped

1 green bell pepper, seeded and thinly sliced

1 lb 5 oz/600 g skinless, boneless chicken breasts, cut into thin strips

scant 1 cup coarsely chopped fresh Thai basil leaves, plus extra sprigs to garnish

2 tbsp Thai fish sauce

cooked rice, to serve

Chicken with Bok Choy
20 minutes to the table

SERVES 4

ingredients

6 oz/175 g head broccoli

1 tbsp peanut oil

1-inch/2.5-cm piece fresh gingerroot,
    finely grated

1 fresh red Thai chile, seeded
    and chopped

2 garlic cloves, crushed

1 red onion, cut into wedges

1 lb/450 g skinless, boneless chicken
    breasts, cut into thin strips

6 oz/175 g bok choy, shredded

¾ cup baby corn, halved

1 tbsp light soy sauce

1 tbsp Thai fish sauce

1 tbsp chopped fresh cilantro

1 tbsp toasted sesame seeds

method

Break the broccoli into small florets and cook in a pan of lightly salted boiling water for 3 minutes, then drain.

Meanwhile, heat the oil in a preheated wok or large skillet over high heat. Add the gingerroot, chile, and garlic, and stir-fry for 1 minute. Add the onion and chicken and stir-fry for 3–4 minutes, or until the chicken is browned all over.

Add the remaining vegetables, including the broccoli, and stir-fry for 3–4 minutes, or until tender and the chicken is cooked through.

Add the soy sauce and fish sauce and stir-fry for another 1–2 minutes, then serve immediately, sprinkled with the cilantro and sesame seeds.

Chicken Curry with Mushrooms and Beans

30 minutes to the table

SERVES 4-6

ingredients

4 tbsp ghee (clarified butter, see
    cook's tip) or 4 tbsp vegetable oil
    or peanut oil
8 skinless, boneless chicken
    thighs, sliced
1 small onion, chopped
2 large garlic cloves, crushed
²/₃ cup green beans
2 cups mushrooms,
    thickly sliced
2 tbsp milk
salt and pepper
fresh cilantro sprigs, to garnish

CURRY PASTE

2 tsp garam masala
1 tsp mild, medium, or hot curry
    powder, to taste
1 tbsp water

method

To make the curry paste, put the garam masala and curry powder in a bowl, then stir in the water and set aside.

Melt half the clarified butter, or ghee, in a large, heavy-bottomed pan or skillet with a tight-fitting lid over medium-high heat. Add the chicken and curry paste and cook, stirring frequently, for 5 minutes.

Add the onion, garlic, and beans, and cook, stirring frequently, for another 5 minutes, or until the chicken is cooked through.

Add the remaining ghee and the mushrooms and, when the ghee melts, stir in the milk. Season to taste with salt and pepper. Reduce the heat to low, then cover the pan and simmer, stirring occasionally, for 10 minutes. Serve immediately, garnished with fresh cilantro.

cook's tip

Ordinary butter burns before it becomes extremely hot, while clarified butter, or ghee, can be heated to a higher temperature without burning. To make clarified butter, melt unsalted butter in a small, heavy-bottomed pan over low heat, until foaming. Skim off the foam from the surface, then drain off the clear (clarified) butter, leaving the milky residue behind. Alternatively, use 3 tablespoons unsalted butter with 1 tablespoon sunflower oil.

Chapter Four

Vegetarian

Spiced Lentil Salad with Goat Cheese

30 minutes to the table

SERVES 4

ingredients

1 tbsp olive oil, plus extra for brushing

2 red onions, finely sliced

2 garlic cloves, crushed

1 fresh red chile, seeded and finely
    chopped

½ tsp ground turmeric

½ tsp ground cumin

½ tsp ground coriander

1 cinnamon stick

2 star anise

5 green cardamom pods,
    gently crushed

1 small piece fresh gingerroot,
    finely chopped

1 cup Puy lentils

scant 3 cups vegetable stock

4 firm goat cheeses with rind
    (chèvre), 3½ oz/100 g each

1 ¼ cups sunblush tomatoes, cut into
    strips

2 tbsp pine nuts, toasted

bunch of fresh cilantro, leaves only

salt and pepper

method

Heat the oil in a nonstick skillet over medium-high heat. Add three-quarters of the onions, and the garlic, chile, spices, and gingerroot, and cook, stirring frequently, for 3–5 minutes, or until the onions are softened.

Add the lentils and stir to coat in the onion mixture, then add the stock, and salt and pepper to taste. Bring to a boil, then reduce the heat and simmer, stirring occasionally, for 15–20 minutes, or until all the liquid is absorbed and the lentils are tender. Remove the cinnamon stick, star anise, and cardamom pods. Let the lentils cool slightly so that they are warm rather than hot.

Meanwhile, preheat the broiler to high. Line the broiler pan with foil and brush with a little oil. Put the cheeses in the broiler pan and cook under the preheated broiler, or until bubbling and brown.

Divide the lentils between 4 individual plates, then scatter over the remaining onion and top with the tomatoes. Carefully lift the cheeses from the broiler pan and arrange on top of the lentils. Scatter over the pine nuts and the cilantro and serve immediately.

Hot Chile Pasta
30 minutes to the table

SERVES 4

ingredients

⅔ cup dry white wine

1 tbsp sun-dried tomato paste

2 fresh red chiles

2 garlic cloves, finely chopped

12 oz/350 g dried tortiglioni

4 tbsp chopped fresh flat-leaf parsley

salt and pepper

fresh shavings of romano cheese,
   to garnish

SUGOCASA

5 tbsp extra-virgin olive oil

1 lb/450 g plum tomatoes, chopped

salt and pepper

method

To make the sugocasa, heat the oil in a skillet over high heat, until almost smoking. Add the tomatoes and cook, stirring, for 2–3 minutes. Reduce the heat to low and cook for 20 minutes, or until very soft. Season to taste with salt and pepper, then pass through a food mill or press through a fine, nonmetallic strainer into a clean pan.

Add the wine, tomato paste, chiles, and garlic to the sugocasa, and bring to a boil. Reduce the heat and simmer gently.

Meanwhile, bring a large pan of lightly salted water to a boil. Add the pasta, then return to a boil and cook for 8–10 minutes, or according to the package directions, or until tender but still firm to the bite.

Remove the chiles from the sugocasa and taste the sauce. If you prefer a hotter flavor, chop some or all of the chiles and return them to the pan. Check the seasoning at the same time, then stir in half the parsley.

Drain the pasta and tip into a warmed serving bowl. Add the sauce and toss to coat. Sprinkle with the remaining parsley, then garnish with the shavings of romano cheese and serve immediately.

cook's tip

If time is short, use ready-made sugocasa, available from most supermarkets and sometimes labeled "crushed tomatoes." Failing that, you could use passata, but the sauce will be thinner.

Eggplant and Bean Curry

20 minutes to the table

method

Heat the oil in a preheated wok or large skillet over high heat. Add the onion, garlic, and chiles, and stir-fry for 1-2 minutes. Add the curry paste and stir-fry for 1-2 minutes.

Add the eggplants and stir-fry for 3-4 minutes, or until beginning to soften. (You may need to add a little more oil since eggplants soak it up quickly.) Add all the beans and stir-fry for 2 minutes.

Pour in the stock and add the creamed coconut, soy sauce, jaggery, and lime leaves. Bring slowly to a boil and cook, stirring, until the coconut has dissolved. Stir in the cilantro and serve immediately, garnished with extra lime leaves if using.

SERVES 4

ingredients

about 2 tbsp vegetable oil or
    peanut oil

1 onion, chopped

2 garlic cloves, crushed

2 fresh red chiles, seeded
    and chopped

1 tbsp Thai red curry paste

1 large eggplant, cut into chunks

4 oz/115 g baby eggplants

1 cup shelled baby fava beans

¾ cup fine green beans

1¼ cups vegetable stock

2 oz/55 g creamed coconut, chopped

3 tbsp Thai soy sauce

1 tsp jaggery or soft light brown sugar

3 kaffir lime leaves, coarsely torn,
    plus extra whole leaves, to garnish
    (optional)

4 tbsp chopped fresh cilantro

Broccoli with Peanuts
20 minutes to the table

SERVES 4

ingredients

3 tbsp vegetable oil or peanut oil

1 lemongrass stem, outer leaves
    removed, coarsely chopped

2 fresh red chiles, seeded and
    chopped

1-inch/2.5-cm piece fresh gingerroot,
    grated

3 kaffir lime leaves, coarsely torn

3 tbsp Thai green curry paste

1 onion, chopped

1 red bell pepper, seeded and chopped

12 oz/350 g head broccoli,
    cut into florets

¾ cup fine green beans

generous ⅓ cup unsalted peanuts

method

Put 2 tablespoons of the oil with the lemongrass, chiles, gingerroot, lime leaves, and curry paste into a food processor, and process a paste.

Heat the remaining oil in a preheated wok or large skillet over high heat. Add the spice paste, onion, and red bell pepper, and stir-fry for 2-3 minutes, or until beginning to soften.

Stir in the broccoli and beans. Reduce the heat to low, then cover the pan and cook, stirring occasionally, for 4-5 minutes, until tender.

Meanwhile, dry-fry the peanuts in a heavy-bottomed skillet, until lightly browned. Add to the broccoli mixture and toss together. Serve immediately.

Zucchini and Cashew Curry

15 minutes to the table

method

Heat the oil in a preheated wok or large skillet over high heat. Add the scallions, garlic, and chiles, and stir-fry for 1–2 minutes, or until softened but not browned.

Add the zucchini and mushrooms and stir-fry for 2–3 minutes, or until tender.

Add the bean sprouts, cashews, chopped garlic chives, and soy sauce, and fish sauce if using, and stir-fry for 1–2 minutes.

Serve the curry immediately, garnished with whole garlic chives.

cook's tip

Try to find small zucchini. If you have to use larger ones, you may need to cut the slices in half before cooking.

SERVES 4

ingredients

2 tbsp vegetable oil or peanut oil

6 scallions, chopped

2 garlic cloves, chopped

2 fresh green chiles, seeded
 and chopped

1 lb/450 g zucchini,
 cut into thick slices

4 oz/115 g shiitake mushrooms,
 halved

generous $\frac{1}{3}$ cup fresh bean sprouts

generous $\frac{1}{2}$ cup cashews, dry-fried

a few fresh garlic chives, chopped,
 plus whole garlic chives to garnish

4 tbsp Thai soy sauce

1 tsp Thai fish sauce (optional)

Spiced Pumpkin and Coconut

25 minutes to the table

method

If you are using a whole coconut, pierce with a skewer to punch a hole in the "eye" of the coconut, then pour out and reserve the liquid from the inside.

Measure the coconut liquid and add water, if necessary, to make generous 1 cup. Add the chile, sugar, coriander, cumin, chili powder, and bay leaves to the coconut liquid and set aside.

Break the coconut in half against a hard, durable surface, then peel half the coconut and grate the flesh on the coarse side of a grater or process in a food processor.

Melt the ghee in a preheated kadhai, wok, or large skillet over medium heat. Add the pumpkin and stir-fry for 1 minute. Add the grated coconut and stir-fry, until the mixture is beginning to turn brown.

Stir in the coconut liquid. Increase the heat and continue to stir-fry until only about 4 tablespoons of liquid are left. Sprinkle with the garam masala and continue to stir-fry, until all the liquid has evaporated. Serve immediately.

cook's tip

If you can't find a fresh coconut, use 4½ oz/125 g dry, unsweetened coconut and stir-fry the pumpkin and coconut in a mixture of 4½ oz/ 125 g creamed coconut dissolved in generous 1 cup boiling water.

SERVES 4-6

ingredients

1 fresh coconut

1 fresh green chile, seeded and chopped

1½ tsp sugar

1 tsp ground coriander

¾ tsp ground cumin

¼ tsp chili powder

2 bay leaves

2 tbsp ghee, or 2 tbsp vegetable oil or peanut oil

1 lb 5 oz/600 g pumpkin, peeled, seeded, and coarsely grated

1 tsp garam masala

Indian Cheese and Pea Curry

30 minutes to the table

SERVES 4

ingredients

about 6 tbsp ghee, or 6 tbsp
vegetable oil or peanut oil
3½ cups panir, cut into ½-inch/
1-cm pieces
2 large garlic cloves, chopped
½-inch/1-cm piece fresh gingerroot,
finely chopped
1 large onion, finely sliced
1 tsp ground turmeric
1 tsp garam masala
¼–½ tsp chili powder
3 cups frozen peas
1 fresh bay leaf
½ tsp salt
½ cup water
chopped fresh cilantro, to garnish

method

Heat the ghee in a large skillet or flameproof casserole with a tight-fitting lid over medium-high heat. Add as many panir pieces as will fit in a single layer without overcrowding the pan and cook for 5 minutes, or until golden brown all over. Remove with a slotted spoon and drain on crumpled paper towels. Repeat, adding a little extra ghee, if necessary, until all the panir is cooked.

Reheat the pan with the ghee. Stir in the garlic, gingerroot, and onion, and cook, stirring frequently, for 5 minutes, or until the onion is softened but not browned.

Stir in the turmeric, garam masala, and chili powder, and cook, stirring, for another 2 minutes.

Add the peas, bay leaf, and salt to taste, and stir well. Pour in the water and bring to a boil. Reduce the heat to very low, then cover and simmer for 5 minutes, or until the peas are tender.

Gently return the panir to the pan. Simmer, stirring gently, until the panir is heated through. Taste and adjust the seasoning, if necessary. Sprinkle with cilantro to garnish and serve immediately.

cook's tip

Panir is an unsalted, mild Indian cheese, but is more like firm bean curd in taste and texture. It can be cut into cubes and cooked without melting.

Chili-Yogurt Mushrooms
30 minutes to the table

method

Melt the ghee in a preheated kadhai, wok, or large skillet over medium-high heat. Add the onions and cook, stirring frequently, for 5-8 minutes, or until golden. Stir in the garlic and cook, stirring, for another 2 minutes.

Add the tomatoes with their juice and stir well, then add the turmeric, garam masala, and chili powder, and cook, stirring, for 3 minutes.

Add the mushrooms, sugar, and salt to taste, and cook, stirring frequently, for 8 minutes, or until the mushrooms have given off their liquid and are soft and tender.

Turn off the heat, then stir in the yogurt, a little at a time, beating vigorously to prevent it from curdling. Taste and adjust the seasoning, if necessary. Sprinkle with cilantro to garnish and serve immediately.

cook's tip

Adding the salt with the mushrooms draws out their moisture, giving extra flavor to the juices.

SERVES 4-6

ingredients

4 tbsp ghee, or 4 tbsp vegetable oil
  or peanut oil
2 large onions, chopped
4 large garlic cloves, crushed
14 oz/400 g canned chopped
  tomatoes in juice
1 tsp ground turmeric
1 tsp garam masala
½ tsp chili powder
1 lb 10 oz/750 g cremini mushrooms,
  thickly sliced
pinch of sugar
½ cup plain yogurt
salt
chopped fresh cilantro and
  cilantro sprigs, to garnish

Mexican Tomato Salad
15 minutes to the table

Method

Put the tomatoes and onion into a large serving bowl and mix well. Stir in the beans.

Mix the chile, cilantro, oil, garlic, and lime juice together in a pitcher, and season to taste with salt and pepper.

Pour the dressing over the salad and toss thoroughly to coat. Serve immediately or cover with plastic wrap and chill in the refrigerator, until required.

variations

You could substitute 2 canned chipotle chilies, drained and rinsed, for the fresh chile, and fava beans for the kidney beans, if you prefer.

cook's tip

You can make this salad in advance and store it in the refrigerator, but let it return to room temperature before serving.

SERVES 4

ingredients

1 lb 5 oz/600 g tomatoes, skinned, seeded, and coarsely chopped

1 onion, thinly sliced and separated into rings

14 oz/400 g canned kidney beans, drained and rinsed

1 fresh green chile, seeded and thinly sliced

3 tbsp chopped fresh cilantro

3 tbsp olive oil

1 garlic clove, finely chopped

4 tbsp lime juice

salt and pepper

Vegetarian Fajitas
25 minutes to the table

SERVES 6

ingredients

2 tbsp corn oil

2 onions, thinly sliced

2 garlic cloves, finely chopped

2 green bell peppers, seeded and
 sliced

2 red bell peppers, seeded and sliced

4 fresh green chiles, seeded
 and sliced

2 tsp chopped fresh cilantro

12 wheat tortillas

8 oz/225 g mushrooms, sliced

salt and pepper

method

Heat the oil in a heavy-bottomed skillet over low heat. Add the onions and garlic and cook, stirring occasionally, for 5 minutes, or until the onions are softened. Stir in the green and red bell peppers, chiles, and cilantro, and cook, stirring occasionally, for 10 minutes.

Meanwhile, dry-fry the tortillas, one at a time, for 30 seconds on each side in a separate skillet. Alternatively, stack the tortillas and heat in a microwave oven according to the package directions.

Add the mushrooms to the vegetable mixture and cook over medium heat, stirring constantly, for 3 minutes. Season to taste with salt and pepper. Divide the vegetables between the tortillas, roll up, and serve immediately.

variation

If you don't like dishes too hot, use 2 fresh chiles instead of 4. The fajitas are good served with plain yogurt or sour cream.

cook's tip

Always wash your hands after handling chiles and avoid touching your lips or eyes. If you have sensitive skin, wear rubber gloves.

Index

A

Asian Seafood Soup 29
Asian-Style Seafood Curry 46
beans
  Chicken Curry with Mushrooms and Beans 72
  Eggplant and Bean Curry 81
  Pork with Mixed Green Beans 65

B

beef
  Grilled Steak with Hot Chili Salsa 60
  Spicy Beef 56
  Spicy Beef and Noodle Soup 16
Broccoli with Peanuts 82

C

cheese
  Spiced Lentil Salad with Goat Cheese 76
chicken
  Chicken Curry with Mushrooms and Beans 72
  Chicken with Bok Choy 70
  Ground Chicken Skewers 66
  Stir-Fried Chicken with Thai Basil 69
Chiles Stuffed with Fish Paste 33
Chili-Yogurt Mushrooms 91
Chorizo Empanadillas 26
clarified butter (or ghee) 72
coconut
  Malaysian-Style Coconut Noodles with Shrimp 50
  Spiced Pumpkin and Coconut 87
corn
  Indonesian Corn Balls 20
crab
  Crab and Cilantro Salad 49
  Spicy Crab Soup 10
Crispy Spring Rolls 15

E

Eggplant and Bean Curry 81
eggs
  Mexican Eggs 24
  Omelet Rolls 12
Empanadillas, Chorizo 26

F

Fajitas, Vegetarian 94
Fish Curry with Rice Noodles 34

G

ghee (or clarified butter) 72
Grilled Steak with Hot Chili Salsa 60
Ground Chicken Skewers 66

H

hake
  Tagliatelle with Hake in Chili Sauce 39
Hot Chile Pasta 78

I

Indian Cheese and Pea Curry 88

L

lamb
  Stir-Fried Lamb 59
lentils
  Spiced Lentil Salad with Goat Cheese 76

M

Malaysian-Style Coconut Noodles with Shrimp 50
Mexican Eggs 24
Mexican Tomato Salad 93
mushrooms
  Chicken Curry with Mushrooms and Beans 72
  Chili-Yogurt Mushrooms 91

Mussels with Mustard Seeds and Shallots 45

N

noodles
  Fish Curry with Rice Noodles 34
  Malaysian-Style Coconut Noodles with Shrimp 50
  Pad Thai 63
  Scallops on Noodles 19
  Spicy Beef and Noodle Soup 16
nuts
  Broccoli with Peanuts 82
  Zucchini and Cashew Curry 85

O

Omelet Rolls 12

P

Pad Thai 63
panir
  Indian Cheese and Pea Curry 88
pasta
  Hot Chile Pasta 78
  Pepperoni Pasta 54
  Tagliatelle with Hake in Chili Sauce 39
Pepperoni Pasta 54
pineapple
  Shrimp and Pineapple Curry 40
pork
  Pad Thai 63
  Pork with Mixed Green Beans 65
pumpkin
  Spiced Pumpkin and Coconut 87

S

salads
  Crab and Cilantro Salad 49

Mexican Tomato Salad 93
Spiced Lentil Salad with Goat Cheese 76
scallops
  Scallops in Black Bean Sauce 42
  Scallops on Noodles 19
shrimp
  Malaysian-Style Coconut Noodles with Shrimp 50
  Shrimp and Pineapple Curry 40
  Wok-Fried Jumbo Shrimp in Spicy Sauce 36
Spiced Lentil Salad with Goat Cheese 76
Spiced Pumpkin and Coconut 87
Spicy Beef 56
Spicy Beef and Noodle Soup 16
Spicy Crab Soup 10
Spring Rolls, Crispy 15
Stir-Fried Chicken with Thai Basil 69

T

Tagliatelle with Hake in Chili Sauce 39
tomatoes
  Mexican Tomato Salad 93

V

Vegetarian Fajitas 94

W

Whitebait with Green Chili Sauce 23
Wok-Fried Jumbo Shrimp in Spicy Sauce 36

Z

Zucchini and Cashew Curry 85